POETRY
for the *Love* of
GOD

POETRY
for the *Love* of
GOD

BOOK 4

B.J. NORWOOD

Poetry for the Love of God
Copyright © 2022 by Bobby Norwood. All rights reserved.

No part of this publication may be reproduced, stored in a retrieval system or transmitted in any way by any means, electronic, mechanical, photocopy, recording or otherwise without the prior permission of the author except as provided by USA copyright law.

The opinions expressed by the author are not necessarily those of URLink Print and Media.

1603 Capitol Ave., Suite 310 Cheyenne, Wyoming USA 82001
1-888-980-6523 | admin@urlinkpublishing.com

URLink Print and Media is committed to excellence in the publishing industry.

Book design copyright © 2022 by URLink Print and Media. All rights reserved.

Published in the United States of America

Library of Congress Control Number: 2022908397
ISBN 978-1-68486-178-1 (Paperback)
ISBN 978-1-68486-179-8 (Digital)

22.10.21

All Aboard

There is a special type of train.
That's now pulling into the station.
It journeys alone a straight and narrow path.
It carries us unto eternal salvation.

You can board this train at once.
No reservation has to be made.
Jesus provided us with the sacrifice.
Your fare has already been paid.

Come ye that labor and are heavy laden.
Come and God will give thee rest.
Give unto God your very worse.
And he will reward you with his very best.

Come all ye that are humble.
Come ye that are meek.
Come unto God he that is strong.
Come unto the Lord ye that are weak.

Come ye that are lowly at heart.
Come and seek ye his glory.
Come ye that are with sin.
Come now and be made holy.

The journey can be hard and long.
But it filled with joy and fun.
Come ye and behold our Lord.
See how many shall become one.

This is a luxury train.
You'll find blessings everywhere.
The walls are fortified with forgiveness.
Each car is carpeted with constant prayer.

It's constructed of absolute faith.
An element that's mightier than steel.
The Holy Ghost is your conductor.
And truth is behind the will.

Righteousness is our head of security.
His strict rules will keep us in line.
He requires your complete submission.
But the outcome will be totally devine.

Some things aren't allowed on the train.
He, through corrections, has to take them away.
He will strip you of all of your sins.
And things that causes us to straw.

He will take away self-gratification.
And whatever wickedness he may find.
He's take away your customs and traditions.
Then he will leave them all behind.

Bring all your cares and problems.
We'll examine them one by one.
We'll fix some and give God the rest.
You'll be completely free when he's done.

Straight ahead is selfishness.
But we will take the bypass.
It matters not what we obtain there.
But it's definitely not going to last.

Further down the track are idol gods.
We will take on but let no one get off.
For as soon as you set foot there,
You will quickly become lost.

When we get to Understanding
There may be a short wait.
This is something we all need to have.
But don't worry, this train is never late.

Next stop will be Denominations.
Will everyone please stay together.
For they will try to separate us.
Each one declaring that it is better.

Soon we'll pass through Prejudice.
It's home to sorrow and shame.
Because of their lack of Godliness,
They can't see we are all the same.

Our next to last stop is Death.
It's just a bump in the road for this train.
We are going to zoom right through,
Without even taking on a stain.

We are coming upon our final destination.
No more stops and no more waits.
You can easily tell when you've arrived.
Just look for the pearly gates.

Be Careful Who You Hear

By now you know God's voice.
Then you know that's not it.
You know that you make the choice.
So just tell Satan to quit.

Be careful of the things that you hear.
Be mindful of who you are listening to.
Sometimes words give rise unto fear.
And fear can dictate what you do.

Some tell of an impending doom.
I too contend that for some it's true.
However, panic should have no room.
For God's children know what to do.

Yes! There are many sorrows down the road.
But this will be our finest hour.
His children willfully share the load.
As he endows us with his power.

Satan and his demons are quite cunning,
In efforts to turn our hearts away.
But it's not time to start running.
God has commanded that we watch and pray.

Walk in the Spirit and be strong.
Give comfort to those who weep!
Provide rest to him who travels alone.
And stand watch over them that sleep.

Know ye not that that which you hear
Can have a direct bearing upon your faith.
So follow in the way he has made clear,
Less ye fall from his holy grace.

We are his daughters and his sons.
Let's be of the same mind and heart.
Let us listen not unto the ones
That seek to keep us apart.

The wicked seek to conquer and divide.
That he may be able to rule the day.
But we, with the love of God on the inside,
Realize that the savior of grace is on his way.

The wolves are deceitful and livid.
They clad themselves as sheep.
Always try their words by the spirit,
Less ye be deceived when they speak.

Return now unto the God of thy youth.
For the hour of redemption is at hand.
Abide daily in all of his truth,
That you may be able to stand!

Harken now unto the Lord's voice.
And him shall ye hear.
Enter into his presence with remorse.
That thy way be made clear!

Blessed To Bless

I thank God for my blessings.
And my blessings are not my own.
God sent them to strengthen my faith.
And to keep my Spirit strong.

I watched him fill my cup.
Then I saw it start to overflow.
He blessed me not that I should boast.
But that to others his love I may show.

With favor he has smiled upon me.
The Lord shall meet my every need.
He has blessed me with harvest.
That others I may feed.

The Lord has filled my barns.
He has flooded my soul with pleasures.
In my heart I hide his word.
And in Heaven I lay up my treasures.

I will bless the Lord with all my soul.
And with all that is within the earth.
To the lost I will show the Savior.
To the lowly I will show worth.

I will bless Jesus on the morning.
I will bless him in the setting sun.
I will bless the Lord when evening is come.
And praise him for all he has done.

I will bless the Lord with all my might.
I will bless him with my off springs.
I will bless him from the mountain top.
Bless the Lord all ye living things.

I will bless the Lord through my giving.
That others comes to share his grace.
I will bless him in the valley.
Bless ye the Lord in every place.

The Lord blessed me with salvation.
His wonders and glory are mine to profess.
Our God spared not his generosity.
And now we are blessed to bless.

Blind

I love the Lord so much.
I always keep my eyes on the prize.
I can ever do a self-examination.
But others I am quick to criticize.

I'm well aware of what I am doing.
And I know I shouldn't commit this sin.
With God so loving, I just say a few hail Marys.
And I'm back in his graces again.

So I engage in constant infidelity.
But look at all the good I do.
I'm sure will overlooks a few indiscretions.
After all, he was once human too!

I've carried the Gospel for many years,
I've led hundreds of souls to God.
So what if I'm I have a few wrinkles.
Haven't I done my part.

I worked hard for all this stuff.
I gathered it all for me and my kid.
I don't have time to worry about the poor.
Let them go and do what I did.

She comes to this church week after week.
And she wears that same old mess.
If she didn't have all of those kids.
Maybe she could afford a new dress.

She has been coming here for a long time.
Yes! And it seems she's struggling still.
Her lights are off and they sit in the dark.
I sure God helps her pay the bill.

I'm afraid to go out sometimes.
In the neighborhood, it's only troubles I see.
Kids are constantly dying in the street.
But what have that to do with me!

I can see people sleeping in the street.
I wonder what it is that they did wrong.
They are so foul and so very nasty.
I could never let them into my home.

So many claim to be Christians.
And say God is stayed on their mind.
But when presented the opportunity to serve.
They will conveniently go blind.

Colored by Jesus

People associate me with a race.
No problem! I'm comfortable within my skin.
But if you think this places me into an echelon.
You really need to stop and think again.

If I must be painted a color,
Then please pass Jesus the brush.
Others can be a bit too abstract.
For their judgement comes in a rush.

Yes! I am among the elite.
But not because of what you see.
It's because of so many wonderful colors.
That Jesus has painted inside of me.

Once I was displeased with my color.
For then I was painted with an ugly sin.
But Jesus took out his brush of grace.
And now I'm beautifully borne again.

People try to paint me into a box.
Everyone thinks they are in the know!
When your harmony is determined by a pigmentation.
It's your true colors that you show.
Some people have tried to color me out.
Whereas, Jesus has always colored me in.
Some have colored me as enemy.
But Jesus has colored ne as a friend.

My friends have colored me up.
Others tend to color me as down.
Jesus colored me with his brush of love.
And with a mind that is sound.

Jesus has colored me strong.
It's more than a conqueror that I be.
I gave resistance unto the strong man.
I watched the strong man flee.

Some painted me as lazy and dumb.
Jesus brushed me over as smart.
For he gave me the insight to know.
That only the pure-hearted will ever see God.

I bore my burdens throughout the day.
And the day is almost done.
Then he brushed over all my sinfulness.
And God has colored me son.

Jesus has colored me as helper.
I'm ready and willing to lend a hand.
Jesus colored me not in error.
But according to his perfect plan.

Jesus has colored me as shepherd.
That I may tend unto his sheep.
He has painted me as watchman.
That I might slumber but not sleep.

He has colored me as farmer.
I gather the harvest and plant the seeds.
Jesus painted me as loving.
I attend to my brother and his needs.

Jesus has colored me with truthfulness.
That my words be not hollow.
He has painted me with his wisdom.
I know now which trail to follow.

He painted me ears of the elephant.
I've learned to listen well.
He painted his word into my heart.
I now have a story to tell.

Jesus colored me with his righteousness.
That my living may not be in vain.
Jesus painted me a mighty armor.
I stand and battle in his name.

He colored me with redeeming blood.
Hidden from memory are all my faults.
Jesus stroked me with his holiness.
That his name I may exalt.

Jesus colored me as forgiving.
That I be not trapped in the past.
He has painted, for me, a Spirit of patients.
That swiftness become not weakness, and I last.

The outward man is subjected to his environment.
The tolls of time are easy to see.
But the beauty that sustains unto life,
Is a composition of colors painted inside of me!

Label me not, for I am of many colors.
They are seasonings unto an abundant life.
I am truly a living masterpiece.
Because I am colored by the hand of Christ!

Don't Write Me Off

Hello over there, you people of God!
I'm here! I'm the young generation.
Why do you just write me off?
Know ye not that I too need salvation.

Please don't thumb your nose up at me.
Because of how I wear my attire.
Help me to see a better way.
Don't just leave me to burn in the fire.

You say you don't understand me.
Guess what! I don't understand you.
You are always talking at me.
When I just need a good talking to.

You say that I'm hopeless.
But what are you thinking of!
I only need what my daddy didn't give me.
I just need a father's love.

You think I don't know where you're coming from.
When you keep saying the same old thing.
I'm not asking you to change your song.
Just find a new way to sing.

I cry out to you for help.
You throw your hands up and say I'm lost.
And I'll probably remain this way forever.
Because you have already written me off!

I don't understand people like you.
Who can so easily give up on folks like me.
But I am the reason for your calling.
If the blind lead the blind who will see!

I can accept you saying I'm lost.
But will you just leave me behind!
Then you should eat your own words.
For if ye seek you will find.

I usually to do things in my own way.
Sometimes it's more than the laws will allow.
You are quick to say I'm not doing things right.
But did anyone care to show me how!

If everything I do is wrong.
Then tell me what you think I should do.
But please keep this thought in mind.
I grew up in a different time then you.

You fill me up with your words.
Most of which, I don't understand.
Can you please show me an example!
Will someone please imitate this Jesus man.

I know you attempt to represent God almighty.
So I assume you to have a good intent.
My days and nights are spent dodging bullets.
Who has the time to stop and repent?

I know I need to take a different path.
Someone should try to show me how.
This sinful road leads only unto death.
I need a change and I need it now!

You say I'm not open to instructions.
That may or may not be true.
How can you know if can be reached?
If you keep ignoring me like you do!

You never come to visit me on lockdown.
Yet you say this man, Jesus, paid your bail.
I guess it's easier to give me the 'big write off'.
And just let me rot in this hell.

What that thing you say about the strong!
How they should be bearing something of the week.
I can't put my finger on the right words.
But I know there's something that I seek.

I see you when you're all dressed up.
And going into that meeting place.
You come out full of smiles and laughter.
That is unto you look into my face.

Can't you see I want joy in my life.
Oh yes, I want to be happy too.
So do I follow after this Jesus guy!
Or should I be just like you.

If is way is so much better than mine,
Then shouldn't some try to let me know.
And if I want to meet this savior of yours,
Can you tell me where I should go?

Tell me, what is his fee!
I might be willing to pay the cost.
But if I'm ever to walk in his freedom.
Then please don't just write me off!

At times I reach out for someone.
But no one always seems to be right there.
Then how can I know this father, son, and Holy guy!
How can I really know that they even care?

Yes! I hear what you have to say.
How am I to know it's not a lie?
I need Holy men to stand before me.
As an example for me to live by.

Hey look! Maybe I'm not your worry!
And maybe you really can't make the time.
I just feel like I'm in the wrong place.
And that God's people ae leaving me behind.

If your time is your own.
Then go ahead and consider me a loss.
But if anything you say about God is true.
Then please, I beg, don't just write me off.

Don't Let Go

Lord, just this morning I was high on you.
But now my Spirit is very low.
Oh God! If you hide yourself from me.
I'll have nowhere else to go.

I went to have counsel with my brother,
But he wasn't anywhere around.
I tried to lean upon a friend.
Again he only let me down.

My soul is in need of something.
What it is I'm not really sure.
I just know that when I have a sickness.
You always have a cure!

Right now it feels like a long journey.
And I fight to bypass the gates of Hell.
I invest my all into this hike.
But without you I will surely fail.

Keep me within thy grasp of mercy, oh Lord!
Please show mercy unto thine own.
Abide thee with thy servant, my Lord.
I don't want to tread this path alone.

No one can pluck me from thine hand.
This, oh Lord, I have come to know.
Let thou favor continue with me, sweet Jesus!
And I beg of thee, please don't let go!

Excited

I'm excited about God being in my life
I'm excited to live out each.
It's a wonder to be love by the Christ
And to walk in his way.

I get excited even when there is trouble.
Because Jesus is a true friend.
And just when they seem to double.
Jesus always brings them to an end.

I get excited that his wisdom keeps me alive.
I get excited by the things that I learn.
The more I know the more I realize
That God knows exactly what he's doing.

You may miss it at first glance.
But look closer and you'll come to understand.
And if you really give faith a chance.
You'll see that Jesus has it all in hand.

Some use theoretical science as an explanation,
For man to maintain an evil heart.
I'm so excited to know that all of creation,
Points back to the presence of God.

I'm so excited that it makes me sing.
His joy conquers my days.
Oh what pleasures my sorrows bring.
When I stop to give God a mighty praise.

I get so excited sometimes that it makes me cry.
When through the eyes, of faith, I see.
That Jesus was purposed to come and die.
Oh what he must have endured just for me.

Wrap your mind around the magnitude of his love.
A love proven to be greater than death.
That had Jesus to come down from above.
And he remitted my sins before my first breath.

There's a party happening in my heart.
Sin and doubt are never to be invited.
If you know the faithfulness of our God,
How can you not be totally excited!

Fall

When I check the pulse of the Church.
There's a scary evilness that I sense.
So many of us haven't made up our minds.
And are content to straddle the fence.

We have a workable knowledge of good and evil.
But are too quick to say 'to each his own'.
God has called us to make a stand.
And either it's right or it's wrong.

You say you can't change the world.
But when did anyone command you to!
God is only asking you to obey him.
So stand up and to God be true.

If you are straddling the fence.
You are of no good to God at all.
So stop holding the fence post.
Just lean back and fall.

Many evildoers are manning the churches.
And we just sit back and grin.
As long as they pay their tithes,
We are willing to overlook their sin.

You made me pastor in this place.
I'm here just to lead you.
No matter how rich God has made me.
You must pay me for all that I do.

We all should have our limits.
I do believe that to be true.
But it's who should be setting those limits.
It's not left to me or you.

Maybe you are the chief deacon!
And the biggest whoremonger of them all.
Then you need to turn loose of the pole.
Then lean back and just fall.

God's word teaches us what is right.
Then why do we easily accept what's wrong.
You say I just live my own life.
And I learned to leave others alone!

I guess to some that may sound well and good.
And it's might just be the easiest way.
I think we should search the scriptures.
And hear what God has to say!

It there's severe pain in my eye,
Do the feet refuse to work anymore!
But when searching for the eye's relief.
I take the whole body to the store.

Get off of the fence and be hot or cold.
God has decreed his people to stand tall.
But God can't use you while on the fence.
Come down even if you have to fall.

It matters not which side you fall on.
Just roll over onto your face.
Pray to God to lift you back up.
He will put you in the proper place.

As exampled by Paul, he can pluck from either side.
But those on the fence will not do.
For God is just about to regurgitate.
The straddled ones are his spew.

Help Wanted

Jobs! Jobs! Jobs! And more Jobs!
That's what we have for you.
It matters not about your education level
Or what type of work you're accustomed to.

We have employed millions,
But there are many slots remaining.
We have a manual that will guide you.
And we have on-the-job training!

The work is not always easy.
But just get a load of the pay!
We supply all the tools you'll need.
And have assistance all the way!

You can choose your own hours.
But it must be in the day light.
For soon the darkness will set in.
And no man works in the night.

Come now and bring everyone you can.
More than will come is what we need.
Some in the barns and some in the fields,
There are so many sheep to feed!

Come all ye that called upon the Lord!
Bring your old, your young, and the new!
Look and see that the harvest is plentiful.
But the committed laborers are few!

Come! Let's tear down these walls.
That we may build barns which are greater.
The Lord is in need of workers today.
For soon there will be no later!

Tear down the walls of hatred.
Dismantle the wall of race.
Destroy the walls denominations.
That lovers of Crist are in one place.

Let's tear down the wall of generations.
Let young and old tarry side by side.
Come shine light into the darkness
And let the wicked not hide.

Let's expand the roof of love
To cover a much larger flock.
But we must be about God's business.
For we are up against the clock.

Come all that have received his love.
Come all with a heart to care.
The work is a long and mighty one.
But the pay is heavenly and fair.

Come ye to plant the seeds
Come ye and let's till the soil.
Come ye to carry the lamp.
Come ye to pour the oil.

Come ye all the tool makers.
Come ye the tools to employ.
Come ye handmaids and husbandmen.
Let's fill the master's heart with joy!

Come ye that are with plenty.
Come now and share the cost.
Come ye lowly and be made watchmen.
For no sheep should be lost.

Bring ye shears of holiness.
That the word may cut away the sin.
Let the sheep graze on grass of righteousness.
That the shepherd may gain a friend.

Some work only when it is sunny.
A few will work through the rain.
Some will fold under the pressure.
Others will baulk at the first sight of pain.

We are in need of those with dedication.
Who will work when it is not any fun.
Those who labor beneath sweat and tears.
And work until the day is done!.

Come in the early morning.
Come ye when the day is noon.
But come now to prepare the harvest.
For the master herder comes soon!

Imitate Christ

Most of us have had our heroes.
Someone that we could aspire to be.
For me no man fills those shoes.
Jesus fulfills all of that for me.

Don't misunderstand, there are those that I respect!
And there are a lot of people whom I admire.
But Jesus is the one that I care to imitate.
He fulfills all that I could ever desire!

I haven't always been so faithful.
But now I'm committed for life.
If you desire someone to emulate.
Let me suggest that you imitate Christ.

Why should you imitate Christ?
Is it because he died, yet, he lives?
Yes! For some that is reason enough.
Also he never takes more than he gives.

Be ye bold in the Lord!
For Jesus was bold without a doubt.
Just ask the men trading in the temple.
Before Jesus chased them out.

Let your heart be filled with the love of God.
Enough to cover even your worse enemy.
Then display that love before others.
That his glory the world might see.

Have something you're willing to die for.
Preferably, the first to die for you.
But first submit unto the will of God.
That your living will be true.

Embody ye the words of the Lord.
And take heed to his advice.
That with this hope in your heart,
You too will pass from death unto life.

Offer peace, therefore, unto every man.
That you make, unto yourself, a brother.
Owe unto each one nothing,
But that you have love, one for the other.

As Christ has blotted out your transgressions.
Let it so be in all of your living.
Learn to leave hatred in the past.
And strive to be more forgiving.

Desire ye a clean and pure heart.
Be thou numbered among the meek.
If you should find that you are the strong.
Then show mercy unto the weak.

If you be a partaker of his grace.
Knowing ye that God has blessed your soul.
Then let his words echo from your mouth.
That others may enter into the fold.

Though I offer myself up as an example.
Of how live a forgiven and righteous life.
At times, I've disappointed even myself.
So I plead with you to imitate Christ.

Infidelity

We made a great commitment.
To each other and unto the Christ.
We built a family together.
While building an incredible life.

We had pains and struggles together.
And we shared much joy through the years.
Then you, Infidelity, came into our lives.
And you left all of us in tears.

So much time and efforts to build this up.
Now infidelity is tarring it all down.
With trust he was all I could see.
Now I don't even want him around.

I know God was once in all of this.
And he and I wanted it to last.
But a broken trust, a broken heart, and infidelity
Are more than I can get past.

I knew from the start he wasn't perfect.
But I thought he was perfect for me.
He says he will always love us.
But that's more than I can see.

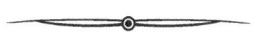

There was once a solid wall.
But infidelity came and made big holes.
Even if I tried to let it go.
It's too late because everyone knows.

Yes! he's a great provider.
And a wonderful father to his kid.
All of my close friends know what happened.
I just can't forget what he did.

I must have my revenge.
He must come to know an equal pain.
He went out and had his fun.
Then came home and brought this shame.

He has totally betrayed me.
It's something I'll make him regret.
I'm not willing to forgive.
And I'll make sure he doesn't forget.

I know Jesus really loves me!
By his blood he has set me free.
If love covers a multitude of faults,
Is one of them infidelity.

Jesus is Right

Blessed is he who hunger and thirst after righteousness.
At least that's what Jesus had to say!
It was true over two thousand years ago.
And it's still true until this day!

I don't see that we have an excuse.
There's no need to go through life being blind.
Jesus has not gone into hiding.
He says to seek him and ye shall find.

Some are stopping just short of his glory.
By accepting darkness rather than light.
They choose to follow after the wiles of Satan.
Without ever putting up a fight.

Jesus way is ever so easy.
And his yoke is always light.
Darwin theorized it all too wrong.
Believe it when I say Jesus is right!

We need to be more and more aware.
That Jesus said to watch and pray.
He warned us of the false prophets.
And other evils to come our way.

Jesus said the world will hate you.
And you will be persecuted for the sake of my name.
The world finds new ways to accomplish this.
But the outcome is evil just the same.

Just stand up for God today.
And see the ease in losing a friend.
But stay mindful of what you have to gain.
Eternal life awaits you in the end.

Be ye steadfast in the Lord, ye of faith!
Continue to reject evil and choose the light.
The Lord is thy true redeemer.
Jesus is Lord and Jesus is right!

Continue then on the straight path.
Though evil may press on every hand.
Obtain strength by waiting upon the Lord.
And you shall be able to stand.

Band together in your love for Christ.
That all the world might also see.
So others might consider a life of servitude.
And others may be set free!

Pray ye also one for the other.
Be ye long in prayer and not cease.
Make your faith known unto God.
That he may fill your heart with his peace.

Stand ye I say and be strong in the Lord.
Let the Spirit of the Lord guide you.
He shall convince and remind that Jesus is right.

Jesus has made the hillsides plain.
He has made the crooked places straight.
He stands at your door and knocks.
Please let him in before it's too late.

Call now upon the name of the Lord.
Unto God, make your partitions be known.
Choose Jesus as your savior, this moment.
Don't wait until the moment is gone!

Choose ye the Lord in this day.
Call upon him in this very place!
Have faith in Jesus, our Christ.
That you may behold his face.

Jesus says he's with us until the end.
So no way will we lose this fight.
Just put on the whole armor of God.
And battle all day, for Jesus is right!

Just Thinking

Occasionally I'll find a place to stop for a while.
Then I'll take a moment to look around.
I wonder if I truly have a real grasp.
Do I know what's going down?

At times I have a handle on things.
Then again I'm not so sure.
There appears to be a new sickness.
And I wonder we'll ever find the cure.

It looks like the righteous are going dormint.
And everything evil seems to win.
The ungodly keep blazing new trails.
And God's people seem to create new sins.

But I tell myself that can't be true.
There's no way that can be done.
Though things seem more and more outrageous.
There's nothing new under the sun.

Like so many that came before me,
I'll like to leave the world a better place.
I want to make a proper contribution.
Before I look God in the face.

I'm not exactly sure what it is.
But there must be more I can do.
There are so many walls to be torn down.
But how am I to ever break through.

I feel strongly that we are running out of time.
It's true for the world and especially for me.
But there are still too many shackles in the world.
So many people still to be set free.

So loudly sinners are crying out.
But no one takes time to stop and hear.
Some Christians are lost in selfishness.
Others are bound by senseless fear.

I can see the hunger and the thirst.
But only a few can I personally touch.
I convince myself that I'm only one person.
And that I can only do so much.

But is this just another excuse?
Have I really done enough?
Have I used the strength of my faith!
Do I push harder when things are tough?

The old and the young are hurting.
At times it shows on their faces.
Am I choosing my words wisely?
Are my efforts in the right places?

So many decisions and choices to make!
I've learned I can't do it on my own.
I'm always met by limitations.
Even when I think I'm being strong.

God desires so much more than this.
Especially from the salt of the earth.
But if the salt has lost it savor,
What then is it worth!

It's our time to serve.
Our day is not yet done.
But as soon as the enemy appears
We want to tuck tail and run.

When I look back I can see gaps.
Where I haven't always done my best.
It's time to let go of the past.
For we now face our greatest test.

Here we are on the frontline.
Getting what may be our last shot.
Are we going to fight our way through?
Are we giving it all that we got?

I was never as strong as Samson.
And my strength is not what it use to be.
But I must stand even unto death.
For our Lord is counting on me.

I will stand up for his righteousness.
I pray I don't have to stand alone.
But be that as it may.
I'll fight until my last breath is gone.

There is no other option.
I don't see that I have a choice.
The Lord is sending out the call.
The blessed, of God, shall heed his voice.

I'm sitting here and just thinking.
There is so much strength and even fun.
If we all would join hands
And fight this battle as one!

Lay Me Down

Lay me down by the water.
And the water will become still.
Lay me down before the war
And watch me do God's will.

Lay me down
And joy shall not end.
Lay me down
And enemies become your friends.

Lay me down in midst of turmoil.
And all your troubles shall cease.
Lay me down around your home
And there shall be peace.

Lay me down
And let me fill the street.
Lay me down
And the hungry shall have meat.

Lay me down
That children might not rebel.
Lay me down
And lock the doors to hell.

Lay me down
So the saddened shall not weep.
Lay me down as shelter
That they find comfort in their sleep.

Lay me down
And the wanderers will have nest.
Lay me down
And the weary shall have rest.

Lay me down
And travel not alone.
Lay me down
And thou shall keep you strong.

To lay me down
Look not very far.
To lay me down
Find me where you are.

Lay me down.
In your heart I'm found.
For I'm God's love,
Lay me down!

Let Go

Having been borne of man and in sin,
I understand the desire to be in control.
But with all my power and strength,
I have not the ability to save my soul.

My thoughts and ways belonged to me.
I carved out a pattern of my own.
It took a whole lot of convincing.
Before I realized that I was wrong.

It was I who set my goals.
I designed and fulfilled my dreams.
Before I could realize it wasn't just me.
They were falling apart at the seams.

At my house, I was in charge.
I say who goes out and who comes in.
Yet I possessed not the power.
To separate my heart from my sin.

I was a fairly well educated man.
In fact, I considered myself to be smart.
It's easy for anyone to change their mind.
But what does it take to change a heart.

I traveled the world here and there.
I went anywhere I wanted to be.
I operated under the distinct illusion.
That I was powerful and free.

But could I end my journey in Heaven?
Just because it's where I want to go.
Could I live life in any way I please.
And still be welcomed at Heaven's door.

Grace sent faith into my life.
I saw that I was not king of the earth.
It made me see that I was wrong.
And that I had been wrong from birth.

After all of the school and the travel.
There were still things that I didn't know!
But if my desire was to get it right.
I would have to let go!

Yes! I could manage me quite well.
But what was to be my final goal.
For I was on the fast track to hell,
Carrying destruction for a beautiful soul.

Where was this change to come from?
Am I already too set in my ways!
Can I voluntarily give up my freedom?
And become one of God's slaves!

How am I to accomplish this new creation.
You can't re-enter the womb on this earth.
Then I heard about God's plan for salvation.
It is equivalent to a new birth.

There I sat deep within my plunder.
And I agonized for hour upon hour.
Could I master this change I wondered.
Where was I ever to get the power.

Does it involve me walking on fire?
Is there some special person I need to know?
Yes! I needed to bring Jesus a sincere desire.
And then I had to learn to let go!

You have to release the remote.
And give Jesus absolute control.
Things will end on a positive note.
When you give Jesus charge of your soul.

I don't know everywhere the journey will take you.
But I have assurance of where it will end.
Acknowledge Jesus in everything that you do.
And see how a savoir becomes a friend!

I hope these words become accepted advice.
For this one thing I've come to know.
That there is so much more to this life.
When we truly learn to let go!.
LET ME BE BORN

Hey out there! pregnant lady.
Hello from the inside.
I'm someone to have and to hold.
Not something you kill just to hide.

Why short I be cut short?
Why can't I get to giggle and smile?
True! No one knows what the future holds.
But I don't to have one as an unborn child.

I don't understand the purpose for killing me.
Is it just to hide your shame!
Then please let me be adopted.
And I'll wear a different name.

So what! I wasn't in your plan!
Is that what this is all about.
I didn't plan this thing either.
But in due time I'll gladly come out.

To have a child or not to have one.
Sometimes people can get a little torn.
I didn't ask to be here.
But I beg of you to let me be born.

Becoming a single parent might be scary.
But it's been done a million times before.
You might be at odds with the other parent.
But killing me will not settle the score.

You may think you don't own much.
And think you have nothing to give.
That may or may not be true.
But don't take away my chance to live.

The abortion might meet with your appeal.
From my perspective it's no damn good.
May I suggest giving faith a try.
And to Hell with Planned Parenthood.

I don't know whose agenda they follow.
But it's definitely not of God.
I could probably do great work for Jesus.
But you choose to stop me before I start.

I don't think I'm asking too much.
I ask not for a pink pony or a unicorn.
I may or may not be anybody important.
But I should have the right to be born.

Some things are illegal and some are not right.
You get to choose which side you are on!
But you take all choices away from me.
What you do is both legal and wrong!

According to the Holy Bible that you read.
'It's appointed unto man once to die.'
But I would like to try live a little first.
At least be given a chance to try!

No child should die such an untimely death.
It shouldn't be a part of anyone's plans.
If a child is to meet an intentional demise.
It certainly shouldn't be at the mother's hand.

I don't care about your education level.
Or what elite status you may adorn.
Just give me a chance at life.
I just want to be born!

I don't care if you have any status at all.
Or how badly you think your life is torn.
Just give somebody a chance to love me!
I just want to be born!

If I'm a product of rape or incest.
You may have fear of being scorned.
But that's not of any importance to me.
I just want to be bore!

You may think you have too many already.
And your nerves are already worn.
I'm here now and there are no suitable options.
I just want to be born!

So you have plans to travel with the band.
It matters not if you play drums or play a horn.
I want a chance to have friends too.
Please let me be born!

Let me come into the world.
I'm not even asking to share your hearts.
I'm not angry if I don't get to know you.
Just don't throw me into the box for spare parts.

You may be torn,
But let me be born!
You may be worn,
But let me be born!

You may be scorn,
But let me be born.
Regardless of what you adorn.
JUST LET ME BE BORN!

Lift

The wicked sought to destroy him forever.
But they were just too blind to see.
He said, "if I be lifted from the earth
I'll draw all men unto me".

So they slew a blameless savior.
But their dream never came true.
Their actions had an adverse effect.
It did the opposite of what it should do.

I imagine the joy they initially felt.
I see them drinking from their victory cup.
I wonder what must have felt.
When they realized that he got up!

What were they to say now!
For Jesus had provided them proof.
Where is the battle now?
How do you fight the risen truth?

They were left to feel the sorrow.
They were now cloaked in shame.
For death could harvest no victory.
Death couldn't even muster a stain.

The method may have changed.
But the principle is still holds true.
Lift up the name of Jesus.
And watch the marvels that he will do.

Lift him with your words.
Lift him in all thy ways.
Praise him in times of joy.
Lift him on your stormy days.

Lift him when you are all alone.
Lift him in the midst of others.
Lift Jesus before your sisters.
Raise him unto your brothers.

Lift Jesus because you are free.
Lift him regardless of the cost.
Praise him among the saints.
Lift him more for those that are lost!

Lift him for the rich and mighty.
Lift him to the poor that begs.
Lift him with your raised hands.
Lift the Lord with your legs.

Lift the Lord with tongues.
Lift him always in your heart.
Lift the Lord with constant prayer.
Lift him with mighty praises unto God.

Lift Jesus with aid from others.
Lift him with or without help.
Lift the Lord with every breath.
Lift the Lord with every step.

Lift Jesus in times of glory.
Lift him in the midst of shame.
Lift the Lord God on high.
And praise his holy name.

Lift the Lord before the strong.
Lift Jesus unto the meet.
Lift Jesus in your home.
Lift him in the street.

Jesus has already set the precedent.
Similar to that of man-made law.
If you will continue to lift.
Jesus will continue to draw.

Morning

The owl enters into her slumber.
There's a new day in the dawning.
The sun issues out her decree.
And creation begins to heed her warning.

The sun sounds the alarm,
As she reveals her gentle side.
The fowls begin to make a stir.
Creatures of the night begin to hide.

Wolves and hounds have ceased to howl.
There's no more weeping in the night.
Morning came and turned the page.
She has turned the table and set it right.

I watch the sparrows take to flight.
Each has charted its own direction.
They soar with the hawks and the eagles.
And never worry about their own protection.

The pond has started to glistens.
Sharing reflections of a brighter time.
The snake has bored a new skin.
And left the old one behind.

The dog and the cat are not at odds.
They seem to have settled the score.
Very patiently they wait together.
Just to see an open door.

The dew sprang up from nowhere.
And gave bath unto the vegetation.
Then it seeps into the ground.
And offers continued consolation.

Something about the morning is refreshing.
As though there was a re-birth.
And all of Heaven shall rejoice.
Because for a brief moment there's peace on the earth!

Not Here

There's a time when the guns don't sound.
And the bullets will cease to fly.
When children play outside without fear.
And mothers have no reason to cry.

There's a time when the world is at peace.
For conflict has come to a blissful end.
A time when I will break my sword.
For my enemy is now my friend.

In that time, we will all know love.
And trampled beneath my feet is my fear.
That time has been predestined by God.
But for now that time is not here.

One day the fog will dissipate.
And all mysteries will be made clear.
The hour, of the Lord, is at hand.
But the moment is yet not here.

There's a day when all men are as one.
We'll join hands and sing God's praise.
And though that moment is not in sight.
It will be here one of these days.

There is a day that the savior will come.
And the dead shall take their rise.
And though they once were blind.
They shall see through different eyes.

There's a most wonderful place called Heaven.
At least that's what I've been told.
I hear it's the home to a savior.
And bares streets that are paved with gold.

It a place of re-assignment.
For the faithful and the few.
It's where old things have been stripped away.
And behold all things are new!

Sometimes I feel that I'm ever so close.
That the overwhelming joy causes me a tear.
Though I'm only one step away,
I realize that Heaven is not here!

One Mission

Why do we burden ourselves with choices?
And trouble our minds with massive decision.
There's no need for tis turmoil.
We only have one mission.

Some people complain, in great fear,
About how the world is today.
But I inquired of the word and my soul.
As to what God might say.

I'm God, of great power and might.
I desire greatly, to put it on put it on display.
I promised to heal your land.
If only the called would repent and obey.

I showered you with mercy.
I sent, unto you, my only son.
I sent you my Spirit of power.
What more should I have done.

I texted you to come out from the world.
And to build a place of your own.
Yet you slobber over the world.
And wonder what went wrong.

You declare that you are serving me.
But it can't be done through politics.
Why don't the saved try to see
That it's just another of Satan's tricks.

The God, of Heaven, lament not over earthly kingdoms.
I'm not concerned with their rise or fall.
For Christ will soon return,
And bring destruction upon them all.

You choose the wicked to rule my people.
And the instruments play only a sad note.
You are convinced this is my will,
But I never told you to vote!

I never said to change man's law.
I sent you to change his mind and his heart.
The laws leadeth not unto salvation.
Nor do they endear you unto God.

It's your righteousness that you choose.
You defy God wherever you're able.
But if you cast your lots unto demons,
You have absolutely no part at God's table.

Your allegiances are not of faith or truth.
They begat only sin and shame.
ALL of my people come through Christ.
They are known, unto me, only by his name!

Base your faith upon Jesus only.
Not your own understanding or how you feel.
And know you not that for centuries,
Even I withdrew from Israel.

I commissioned you to tend the flock.
To gather the harvest and feed my sheep.
Because of your disobedience and worldly distractions,
I watch them die in the street.

I sent you out to build bridges.
Then you decided it's best to build walls.
But that which is done unto me,
You do unto the least of all.

You serve me with your lips.
And support evil with your life.
But the mind that should be within you,
Is the holy mind of Christ!

You listen to present day Pharisees and Sadducees.
And follow after things not true.
But the same spirit given unto the Apostles,
I also gave unto you!

Turn ye now from the world.
And sincerely seek my face.
Follow after Christ and bot man.
And prove the earth a better place.

Build, unto God, holy cities.
Render unto Caesar only what is due.
Lift the name and body of Christ.
This is what I require of you!

Be not concerned with the shaping of man's kingdoms.
Become a holy and living sacrifice.
For you are given only one mission.
And that mission is Jesus Christ!

One Way

Let God word be your instruction.
Yet this I feel I must say!
That when searching to know God,
There is only one way!

Regardless of your opinion of me.
Or of what you may hear in life,
There's only one way unto God.
And that way is through Jesus Christ.

We can try our best to change things.
But there is no back door.
God did not give us a multiple choice.
He's the same yesterday, today, and forever more.

I understand the desire to change things.
To accommodate ourselves, love ones, or a friend.
But we must align ourselves with the word.
For faith in Jesus Christ is our way in.

I offer no apology for the truth.
But Christ is indeed your only way!
Now we have the choice to make.
And I hope we choose Jesus today!

Jesus is the only name given under Heaven.
Whereby man might be saved.
We can't just change God's word,
To justify how badly we've behaved.

Many people will misrepresent the Gospel.
Knowing that there is no truth in what they say!
It matters not what attention we garnish unto ourselves.
Jesus Christ is still the one and only way!

The irony is still astounding to me.
How we just refuse to let Jesus in.
But we now use the word of God
To justify the acceptance of sin.

Yes! Jesus told us to love all mankind.
And today that command holds true.
But he never said to accept or glorify their sins.
I can love men without loving what they do.

Jesus said for us to abstain from sin.
Then even its appearance we should avoid.
You can make it seem noble if you like.
But sinners and saint are never of one accord.

Sometimes the lines appear to be blurred.
But the difference is like night and day.
However, what Christ taught goes unchanged.
And Jesus only is our one way!

Why lend your support unto evil?
Does it appear to be noble and nice?
I believe we should teach, live, and indeed walk
Only in the ways of Christ!

Please evict self out of your heart.
Make room for Jesus to come in.
I promise new life will truly come.
But only when you are dead to sin.

Please give your entire life unto Jesus.
And behold the dawning of a new day.
When you will stand and declare unto the world
That Christ is indeed our one way!

Pass Me Not

I seek not my own pleasures, oh Lord.
Make known, unto me, thou desire.
The flames of righteousness appear to dwindle.
Use me to help restart the fire.

Thou has blessed me with meadows.
But how many sheep have I fed!
I cannot commit my brother's heart.
But I will follow as I am led.

If you desire someone to minister in prison.
Then I promise to go there too!
It's not my will but thine, oh Lord!
I avail myself completely unto you!

You need someone to go into the streets!
Well Lord that's not my first choice.
But faith will decrease my fears
And I will harken unto your voice.

Maybe I stand to lose a lot
The dangers are easy to see.
But if I should lose it for you.
You promised to return it unto me.

I shall run and not get weary.
Help me to walk and not faint.
Lord help to keep my battery charged up
And to have plenty of gas in the tank.

I desire to serve you, Jesus.
It matters not as to where!
Give me your **G**od **P**ositioning **S**pirit.
To show me how to get there!

Purposed

Let me tell you this truth.
And you can take it for what it's worth.
There have been millions of accidental deaths.
But never one accidental birth.

Regardless of your place of birth,
Nor does it matter about the season,
But if you have ever taken one breath,
Then believe me you have a reason.

Your journey may one of far off.
Or maybe you're needed somewhere near,
But God has given you a soul
And a purpose for being here.

Some are borne to be a whisper.
Some are placed here to hollow.
Some are pre-ordained to take the lead.
But all are borne to follow.

Some are borne out of wedlock.
Some are borne because of a prayer.
But all are borne because of God.
Trust him if you dare!

Some are borne with a silver spoon.
Some God gave unto the poor.
But none has seen or even heard,
All the things God has instore.

I was borne slightly overweight.
Others were borne a bit too thin.
We were all borne with a specific purpose.
Even though we were all borne into sin.

Some were borne without sight.
Others were borne without sound.
Regardless of our perceived shortcomings,
God still wanted to have us around.

Some are here just to be a flicker,
While, others are here to shine.
Some are walking within their purpose.
While other's, their purpose, have yet to find.

Let's all look up and live.
For it's not yet our dying season.
God has ordained for you a purpose
And Jesus holds your reason.

We are destined to live forever.
Whereas, Jesus was predestined to die before birth.
But it was inside of his death
That each life finds it's worth.

Never think you are here by mistake.
For God long ago made his plan.
He designed for each of us a purpose.
Then placed the key into Jesus's hand.

Seek now and ye shall find.
Make this your hunting season.
Find your rightful place in the Lord Jesus.
And there you'll find your reason.

Reaching Out

Many people are there reaching out.
And some don't even understand why.
The soul has an innate desire to live.
No soul really wants to die.

There are reaching out to us.
Will we take the time to see?
That so many souls are in wander.
There are so many souls yet to be free.

Some reach out with anger or confusion.
Others maybe with just a simple smile.
But there is something they see in you.
That tells them you are God's child.

They hear without even listening.
And garble up every word that you say.
They are watching your every step.
Sometimes hoping you show them the way.

Some fear putting themselves out on a limb.
For others it could be a matter of pride.
It's not your worldly possessions that they seek.
They need what you have on the inside.

We take God's gifts for granted at times.
Maybe because we've had them for so long.
And if the world takes awe with us,
We wonder what we have done wrong.

You see! God has saved you.
It's like he placed a light into your heart.
Light has a way of attracting things.
You fuel up on Jesus and light will do its part.

The light doesn't shine into your face.
Yet it lets off a bit of a glow.
And when you really love the Lord.
Somehow it will always seem to show.

This is why you should choose your words carefully.
And always be mindful of each step.
A sinner is searching for someone to believe in.
And he just might need your help.

I realize that we have gone pass this.
But let's get back to the days of yea and nay!
Because our words and deeds reflect the light
That is needed to show someone the way.

Do not be ashamed of the Gospel.
Don't hide the light, let it shine.
Be sure to always walk in the spirit.
And let God be stayed on your mind.

Devote each day to serving God.
And let Jesus set the pace.
Soon you'll see a chance to serve God.
It will be staring you right in the face.

At times the chances seem to be huge.
Sometimes they appear so very small.
But it's nothing God haven't prepared you for.
Just be willing to give God your all.

You see, God has equipped those that he called.
He gave us the strength and the clout.
Now he expects us to extend our hearts.
And give aid to those who are reaching out.

Surrounded

I peer out over the horizon.
The Lord has been my strong tower.
His grace has granted me assurance.
His Holy Spirit has bestowed power.

I see enemies encamped all about me.
They've journeyed from every direction.
They lie in wait to destroy my soul.
But the walls of faith sustain my protection.

I can see jealousy close by,
As she joins forces with hate.
Slander is in communion with deceit.
They make camp outside my front gate.

To the left are worldly pleasures.
They spring up like thorns, from the ground.
Sometimes they dress up as friends.
They serve only to tear me down.

To the right are lusts and temptations.
They followed me from my youth.
Just beyond, I see tall tales,
Trying to block me from the truth.

I can see the wolves of denomination.
They are attired in sheep clothes.
They have darkened the eyes of many.
But they conquer not my soul.

In the rear, I see mighty demons.
They carry the evils of my past.
They desire to overcome my salvation.
I fear not though their approach is fast.

They enter not into my sanctuary.
Because forgiveness has fortified that wall.
They launch their greatest offense.
I honor the Lord as they fall.

The demons breach not my wall.
Therefore, many has taken to the air.
But I wear the whole armor of God.
And I've come to know he power of prayer!

The Holy Spirit keep taking me higher.
While his grace keeps me grounded.
His love keeps filling me up.
And his angels keep me surrounded!

Talents

Some talents may seem derivative.
And maybe some are from birth.
But they are all given by God.
Let's use them for what they are worth.

Remember to display your talents.
Even if no one notice but you.
Do all for the glory of God.
You'll be surprised by what he'll do!

Every good and perfect gift is from God.
Make every effort to give them back.
Just follow Jesus with your gifts.
He will keep you on the right track.

It is not a big mystery.
It's no secret to how this plays out.
With God you reach your potentials.
If you just trust and never doubt.

You could search for your talent.
But seek ye the Lord first.
God will magnify your talent.
As he quenches that hunger and thirst.

I know not the number of your talents.
It may be one, ten, five, or three.
Just give all you have unto the Lord.
And become all that you can be.

There He Goes Again

I'll tell again and again,
For all that it is worth.
God has truly blessed me.
He has since before my birth.

Yes! He blessed me that first time.
Before I could praise him, he blessed me twice.
When I take a long hard look,
He blessed me from here back to his sacrifice.

How do I let him know?
That I feel it's more than I deserve.
Because of his kindness and his deity,
I dedicate my life to serve.

Could it be a mighty love?
That causes Jesus to behave this way.
Then he must have an abundant supply.
For he blesses me every single day!

He blessed me on my way out.
Just as he had on my way in!
I bowed my head and gave him thanks.
I opened my eyes, in time, to see him bless me again.

He blessed me in the morning!
Jesus has blessed me in the night.
He has blessed me out of the darkness.
And blessed to walk in his marvelous light.

Jesus blessed me when I was young.
And even now that I am old.
Jesus has assured me of even more blessings.
When the final story is told.

At my bed side, the doctor said it was over.
My times on earth came to its end.
But just then Jesus stopped by.
My gentle praise was, there he goes again!

Thought of You

Hello my ole and dear friend.
I haven't heard or seen you in a while.
Just wanted to know if you're ok.
Hope this message catches you with a smile.

I allow myself to stay busy most of the time.
But I thought of you again on today.
So I decided to take some time out.
And try to send some love your way.

I know you were troubled a while back.
By some things you were going through.
Just wanted to know if things were better now.
Or if maybe there's something more I can do.

I know we've had our squabbles in the past.
But, in the past, ley's leave them there.
Today has overtaken all of that.
Now you should know that I still care.

I hope you are not holding on to past things.
There's no reason to feel guilty.
You see I'm called upon to forgive.
Just as God has forgiven me!

Please let little spats be as water under the bridge.
That flowed away down the stream.
Let nothing separate us from the love of Christ.
And we both fall short of a dream.

I dream of an eternity with the Lord.
And I pray you will be there too.
I refuse to let misunderstandings hinder me.
And let not Satan use me to hinder you.

If you have need of me,
You know I'll be right there!
Rather it's a joy or a burden,
You know I'll help you share.

There's a love that God gives us.
And it's just too big to hide.
I know it covers all of my faults.
And it conquers my selfish pride.

I asked God what he needed from me.
What other deed it was I could do.
I asked who could I love on today.
And suddenly I thought of you!

Unaware

You thought about giving alms to that stranger.
But you weren't sure if you really should.
Would he use your kindness for evil?
Could your meager amount do any good?

This may be another chance to worship.
A way to express to God that you really care.
God's word has given us warning
That many have entertained angles unware.

She's long on items and short on money, at the register.
She's wasting your time and testing your nerve.
But could she be just another angel.
Giving you another opportunity to serve.

We all travel the roads from time to time.
And we have been made aware of the danger.
It doesn't always turn out so good.
When we give aid to a stranger.

Do I dare recommend you do as I do?
However, I need this to be made clear.
Are we exempt from serving God?
Because Satan discourages us through fear.

Are we really of great faith?
Is it greater than our fear of danger.
Do we just pretend that we don't see?
And bypass what could be an angel.

I'm not the one to decide this for you.
Let your faith make that call.
But I've learned to trust God in some.
And I've learned to trust him in all.

There's an angry old man living next door.
He's always screaming and bothering you.
But how would you feel as an angel,
With no one to ever talk to.

He's just another alcoholic on the street.
You really wish he was gone!
But is he another one of God's angels.
Trying to show you the way home.

So always follow after Christ.
Keep God forever on your mind.
Remember to walk daily in his love.
You may encounter an angel at any time.

Under Contract

I promised that I would bless.
And that's just what I will do.
But the more I give to thee,
The more that is required of you!

Yes! Blessings will I pour out.
Not to boost your selfish ways.
But as investments back into my kingdom.
That other may sing my praise.

Why seek thee full pay.
For service every now and then.
Your faith is a signed contract,
To hold out unto the end.

I will supply all of the materials.
And ye work while it is day.
But if the contract is broken,
There shall be no further pay!

You are under contract with the father.
Seek not thy glory elsewhere.
Render thy labor unto God.
And he shall pay that which is fair.

Yes! I shall reward them.
If, my face, they will diligently seek.
I will reward a total commitment.
The pay is not week to week.

Seek ye the kingdom of Heaven.
Make Jesus into your delight.
Concentrate on rendering him pleasures.
And he will do that is right.

I will be thou Lord and master.
Your sugar daddy I shall not be.
Glory not in the things I've given,
But find your joy in me!

You hide not your heart from God.
It has made known all your desires.
You have partitioned your fulfillment.
But know you what God requires.

Use It For Christ

OK! Now let me deal with you.
In the same manner that God dealt with me.
That is to release your guilt or shame.
And allow yourself to be absolutely free.

Never feel you have more than you deserve.
But in reality we all do!
Just call it his benevolent grace.
Be thankful he gave it unto you!

Regardless of how much you're blessed with.
Let your gift, within your service, be reflected.
Remembering that unto whom much is given,
Much is, in return, also expected.

Maybe you could view it similar to tithing.
But more like an offering I would say.
Please keep your heart and mind open.
For the more you get the more you need to give away.

Never cherish your gifts
More than the one that gave.
For though you are to be a blessing to others.
You also must he save.

God expect your best with one talent.
Expectations are greater when you have ten.
Just sow every seed that you got.
And gather the harvest when the crop comes in.

Harbor not envy for your brother.
When it seems he has enough and to spare!
For God administers out his portions.
And renders unto his children in a way that's fair.

There is no one mighty in his sight.
No special accommodations made for the elite.
He that is thought to be strong,
Must give aid and comfort unto the weak.

Don't forget that we are one body.
With positioned at the head.
The entire body will be strong and prosper.
If, by him, we are willing to be led.

Your talents may be many or few.
Your gift may be great or small.
Good and perfect things are from God.
Forever be willing to offer unto him your all.

Yes, Lord! / I Will

This is not classified information.
Many times, in the past, I have confessed.
That since Jesus came into my life,
I have been magnificently blessed!

I find no shame in praising Jesus.
Nor in calling upon his holy name.
But if my circumstances were different.
Would my dedication be the same!

Recently, God asked me this question.
And it came as quite a blow!
I had to search deep within myself.
So that I may truly know.

How do you let things effect you?
What if I earned a million dollars a day!
Would I continue to give God praise?
Could I continue to walk in his way?

What if wake up on tomorrow
And all that I have was gone!
Would I bow to my knees and give thanks?
Or ride the pity bus and sing a Sad song.

Superficially, my mind went to the story of Job.
And all of the trials that he went through.
Just off the cuff, my answer would be,
If job did it, I can do it to.

That can easily be wishful thinking.
But what was the real truth!
For in reality, I am not Job.
And nor am I Ruth.

It took me a while to answer the Lord.
I'm sure you smiled and asked why!
My life I gave faithfully unto the Lord.
But have I been living a lie!

Do I love the Lord for himself?
Or do I love what the Lord can do?
You see! God already knew the answer.
But he felt I needed to know too!

My mind went back to my youth.
When I knew for sure that I was poor.
When I saw stars through holds in the roof.
And saw the ground through holds in the floor.

Sure God was blessing us back then.
But not what I considered his most choice.
However, that's when Jesus entered into my life.
It was then, I first heard his voice.

You see! Jesus carried me from there.
To where I am this very day.
But what if circumstances changed.
And went back the other way.

It easy to praise God from a mansion.
That sits atop of a plush ridge.
But could you lift your hands in praise?
If you slept beneath a noisy bridge.

After during some soul searching.
Lord, I know I can truly say.
I am in this for you oh Lord!
And I'm in it all the way.

Lord, we are now of the same accord.
You loved me when I had not breath.
And I have loved you, oh Lord!
Before thou blessed me with wealth.

I commit my heart to you, Jesus.
I love you with all of my life.
I will not let depth nor height,
Separate me from the love of Christ.

If thou withdraw thy blessings.
Will I serve and thee still?
I thank you God that I can truly say,
YES LORD I WILL.

www.ingramcontent.com/pod-product-compliance
Lightning Source LLC
LaVergne TN
LVHW011731060526
838200LV00051B/3125